MILLENNIAL TEETH

Crab Orchard Series in Poetry
Open Competition Award

T0170249

Millennial Teeth

POEMS BY DAN ALBERGOTTI

Crab Orchard Review &
Southern Illinois University Press
Carbondale

Copyright © 2014 by Dan Albergotti
All rights reserved
Printed in the United States of America

17 16 15 14   4 3 2 1

The Crab Orchard Series in Poetry is a joint publishing venture of
Southern Illinois University Press and *Crab Orchard Review*. This
series has been made possible by the generous support of the Office
of the President of Southern Illinois University and the Office of the
Vice Chancellor for Academic Affairs and Provost at Southern Illinois
University Carbondale.

Editor of the Crab Orchard Series in Poetry: Jon Tribble
Judge for the 2013 Open Competition Award: Rodney Jones

Library of Congress Cataloging-in-Publication Data
Albergotti, Dan.
[Poems. Selections]
Millennial teeth : poems / by Dan Albergotti.
    pages ; cm. — (Crab Orchard series in poetry)
ISBN 978-0-8093-3353-0 (pbk. : alk. paper) — ISBN 0-8093-3353-8
(pbk. : alk. paper) — ISBN 978-0-8093-3354-7 (ebook) — ISBN
0-8093-3354-6 (ebook)
I. Title.
PS3601.L3343A6 2014
v811'.6—dc23   2014001327

Printed on recycled paper. ♺

The paper used in this publication meets the minimum
requirements of American National Standard for Information
Sciences—Permanence of Paper for Printed Library Materials,
ANSI Z39.48-1992. ∞

CONTENTS

Three

ACKNOWLEDGMENTS

Many thanks to the editors of the publications in which the following poems, some in slightly different forms, first appeared or were reprinted:

32 Poems: "A Theater near You" (as "Coming Soon")
Barn Owl Review: "The Days of Our Lives"
Barrow Street: "Invocation"
Best of the Net 2011: reprinted "Apology in Advance"
Cave Wall: "The Gods Have Given Up on Immortality," "He Believes He Is Some Sort of Savior," "Surprising the Gods," and "What I Wanted to Tell Her about Hell"
The Cincinnati Review: "What They're Doing"
Connotation Press: "Apology in Advance" and "Ghazal for Children"
Copper Nickel: "These Be Hectoring Large-Scale Verses"
Crab Orchard Review: "Holy Night"
DIAGRAM: "December 25, 2005"
Exit 7: "Gloria Patri"
Five Points: "Neither"
The Greensboro Review: "Dusty Field, Dog Barking" and "Years and Years and Years Later"
Grist: "Aubade" and "God"
The Hampden-Sydney Poetry Review: "Chapter One, Verse One" and "Ghazal of Air"
Lake Effect: "Christina Sestina"
The Louisville Review: "Exeunt Voltemand and Cornelius" and "Ghazal of Days"
Lyric Poetry Review: "Infamy"
Memorious: "Inside"

Mid-American Review: "What Everyone Knows"

Pushcart Prize XXXIII: Best of the Small Presses: reprinted "What They're Doing"

roger: "Ghazal for Buildings"

Southern Humanities Review: "No Beginning"

The Southern Review: "Ars Poetica"

storySouth: "Anecdote of the Plate," "Aphelion & Aphasia," and "Disorder"

Terminus: "Splinter & Sneeze"

The Use of the World (Unicorn Press, 2013): several of the poems appear in this limited-edition chapbook

I also thank the Bread Loaf Writers' Conference, Coastal Carolina University, the Hambidge Center for the Creative Arts and Sciences, the Sewanee Writers' Conference, the South Carolina Arts Commission, and the Virginia Center for the Creative Arts for grants, fellowships, and scholarships that supported the conception, drafting, and revision of many of these poems.

I owe great debts to my teachers for their insight and guidance: Fred Chappell, James Dickey, Stuart Dischell, Christine Garren, Alan Shapiro, and Natasha Trethewey.

Many thanks to Rodney Jones for selecting this collection in the Crab Orchard Series Open Competition and to Jon Tribble, Allison Joseph, Karl Kageff, Barb Martin, Wayne Larsen, Bridget Brown, and everyone at the *Crab Orchard Review* and Southern Illinois University Press for their extraordinary work.

Thanks to all my friends in poetry, too many to list, for your sustaining spirit. Among these, I must name Terry Kennedy, Doug Van Gundy, Rhett Iseman Trull, Katrina Vandenberg, Colin Cheney, Nicky Beer, Brian Barker, and Julie Funderburk. Thank you for being family.

Thank you, Jake Adam York, for setting the bar so damned high and for always turning back to extend a hand to me. I miss you, my brother.

And infinite gratitude to my wife, Holley Tankersley, for miraculously converting this intolerable world into a kind of Eden every day.

One

NEITHER

Her eyes flared like torches. She couldn't understand
how she'd struck me dumb. She couldn't believe,
she said, how I could believe nothing, wouldn't accept
that I would choose annihilation, death over life.

(That's what she said: *death over life*. Said it was a choice.)
She told me her lord stood and knocked and waited
for me to open a door. *It's really a simple choice*, she said.
Everlasting life or eternal death. Which one do you want?

Her eyes flared like torches carried by monks
or by villagers. Her words seemed to float
from her mouth, and her teeth were beautiful.
Isn't that strange, that teeth can be beautiful?

Have you ever looked at a mouth and thought,
Those teeth are beautiful? Have you ever looked at a skull
and thought, *Those teeth are beautiful?* Have you ever thought
about the teeth of a crocodile tearing at the flesh

of an early mammal, crushing bones and flashing white
against primordial mud millennia before the first hominid?
Have you ever thought about all those years of silence?
I didn't want to hurt her as she stood there waiting.

I wanted to say something that would please her,
but I couldn't tell her she was right. She was not right.
She was neither right nor wrong, neither light
nor dark. She was neither angel nor demon, neither dove

nor asp. She was neither the one who could save me
nor the one who could damn me. She was neither
the pearl nor the meal, neither the fossil nor the fir.
She was neither judge nor gem, neither catechism

nor catacomb, neither breath nor body nor fire nor fear
nor yes nor no. She was neither nil nor love
in this half-life world, neither the bomb, nor the flash,
nor the wave that washes everything away.

Well? she said, nearly spitting, her eyes flaring still.
Which . . . one . . . do . . . you . . . want?
And my answer held there, like a flame,
in the deepening silence between us.

APOLOGY IN ADVANCE

I tried to do it in one voice.

We've been over this before.

It was as orderly and complete
as my mother's cross-stitch sampler—
the Governor's Palace in colonial Williamsburg
and the whole goddamned alphabet—
framed by my father at the foot
of the staircase. As flat and even
as the layer of dust that collected
on the top of that frame, on top
of her glossy coffin's lid.

It made a sort of sense.

It was not this world.

INVOCATION

O lord
of severed cord
and flesh, lord of fever,
sweat, dementia, and meat cleaver,
lord of curtains set ablaze, of burning,
lord of tumors, of remission, of returning,
lord of time and time alone, lord of space and empty space,
lord without body, without soul, lord without feet or face,
lord of statistics, lord of bodies, lord of death,
lord of breathless hope, lord of hopeless breath,
O lord of every deafened ear,
I know you'll never hear
in vacant air
this prayer.

CHAPTER ONE, VERSE ONE

In the beginning was the word,
and the word was *no*.
And the word trembled out
over sand and snow.

Over seas and mountains
the word was spread.
Over clay and ash,
remains of the dead.

In the beginning was the word,
and the word was a lie,
and that lie lay hard
under a darkening sky.

Through wind and rain
the word echoed still.
Through wet summer air
and dry winter chill.

In the beginning was the world,
and it called for a word
with each great crashing wave,
each still, stiffened bird.

Where still bodies lay
and time would defile,
the world needed a word
to help nurture denial.

In the end the word
was only a sound,
a sound no one hears
beneath grass or mound.

You can still hear it now,
endless echoes of *no*.
And still blows the sand,
still falls the snow.

APHELION & APHASIA

July, Virginia, one hundred degrees.
A wall of wind has swept enormous trees
off the face of the earth, and a sick man
has killed twelve strangers in a theater,
and I'm supposed to craft an art from air—
make something here worth memory, worth speech—
and I just want to make a confession:
I can't frame, form, or even find those words.
Syllables stutter in my silent head
while the distant sun spits its light at me
eight minutes, twenty-five seconds ago.

This morning I tried to articulate
a rough definition of poetry
to a table of strangers. I told them
essentially nothing. It was mostly
pauses, unfinished sentences, silence.

One evening during a broadcast bombing
of Baghdad in the nineties, my sister,
whose mind had not yet completely fallen
into madness, tried to describe for me
the sound of a tremendous explosion
I had missed while I was in the bathroom.
Boom! she said, and her eyes grew wide, her head
bobbed back a bit, and then she stared, confused,
at the blank space before her, as if stunned

by the percussive force of her own voice
or baffled by its inability
to make any meaning, to say it right.
Wow, I said, trying to offer comfort.

We'd each managed one simple syllable,
and that's the only real conversation
I can recall over the void of years.

When I was leaving the family slowly,
my mother would call and ask, *How are you?*
I would say, *Fine,* and we would both listen
to the silence on the line, and I would
listen to the silence of my bedroom
in Greensboro after she had hung up
in Florence, would imagine the silence
of that house that I'd abandoned her to,
the silence she would sleep in and wake to.

In her last few years, she lost more and more
the ability to speak. *Right, right, right*
was almost all she could say in response
to anything.

       Mother, I can't come home.

Right, right, right.

       Mother, I won't be coming
home ever again. I'm gone.

       Right, right, right.

Mother, I wish it could have been different.

Right. It could have been. *Right.* It couldn't have.
Right.

  The last time I saw her in this world,
she'd been diagnosed with early stages
of Alzheimer's. I sat at a table
with her and my father, not having seen
either for months. I remember nothing
of the conversation except for this:
her slow struggle to construct one sentence.
It's only . . . going to get . . . worse.
          Right, right, right.

Composers, painters, and sculptors waited
patiently as I tried to find the words.
But I was hearing the meter of words
unsaid, the silence between my attempts
feeling closer to poetry, to truth.

I looked beyond them and out the window
at the torn limbs that still littered the ground
after the great storm of two weeks before.

Dante's suicides are denied the right
to speak, transformed into small trees that sway
in hell's wind. They must be injured again
to gain a momentary voice. They speak
when Dante breaks their branches, and like most
of the souls in that inferno they use
their allotted time to express regret.

My voice felt as wrong as the distant sun
warming the earth when it's farthest away
as I stammered about form, refinement
of the soul, the transformative power
of metaphor, and the necessity
of failure. I smiled and excused myself.

I walked outside amidst the fallen limbs
and listened hard to their silence, trying
to imagine the sound of the great wind
that passed two weeks before I'd arrived there,
feeling the heat of the far sun, knowing
it took eight minutes, twenty-five seconds
to reach me, knowing that what's in the past
is unreachable now and all voices
will be quiet forever soon, fading
as they get farther and farther away.

HE BELIEVES HE IS SOME SORT OF SAVIOR

He does.
He says he was
in one of his other
lives son of a virgin mother
and a father whose heart was rough as God's.
He says his father taught him how to fear a rod's
swift arc through the air above his back. *Now he's dead,* he says.
The therapist indulges such stories, his excesses.
It's part of getting well to craft outlandish tales,
she thinks, more healthy than those caustic wails,
the desperate rending of his soul.
He says he can control
the tempest waves.
He saves.

AFTER THEBES

If it were true that the loss of one sense
led to the enhancement of the others,
and if you had plucked out your own eyes
after learning the truth of a life,
would the shifting sand beneath each step
as you walked away along the desert road
become a comforting drone, that fine crush
like ground glass? Would the taste of water
on your parched lips become bitter or sweet,
like a father's blood or a mother's tongue?
Would the occasional smell of rotting flesh,
carrion on the roadside, make you feel less alone?
Would a cool evening breeze on your arm
become the blessed touch of an older woman?
In this darkness, would you begin to see
the use of the world and learn to make yourself
something else, something strangely new,
and be able to wholly forget ever having been
anyone's child, any mother's son?

SURPRISING THE GODS

Suppose Eurydice, running through the evening field,
had stepped on the adder as planned, but it was the adder
that died, Eurydice's heel coming down on its upper vertebra
and snapping it at once. Imagine her stooping down,
staring in wonder as the serpent twitches in small throes.
What would the gods do with that? How would they rewrite
the story that must be told? And would they question themselves
as they recovered from their surprise, as they made her
in some other way the impossibility she became
the moment her beauty first made Orpheus sing?

DUSTY FIELD, DOG BARKING

When I try to see my mother in this world,
standing in a dusty field, confused
and taking tentative steps like a child— .

when I try to see her there, after
she's climbed out of the car she'd driven
over the shallow ditch miles from home—

when I try to see her there, wondering
why she's not at the store or home,
maybe wondering where her son is—

when I try to see her there,
I can hear nothing
but small birds in high branches

and the distant barking of a dog
at the edge of an unseen fence.
He's heard the wheels' thump, creak

of old shocks, maybe the horn. He's barking
at what he can't see. When I try to see
my mother there, I hear the barks

becoming fainter, more intermittent
as the dog begins to understand
that nothing's happened, no one's coming.

GHAZAL FOR BUILDINGS

What has fallen? A building.
What has fallen now? Another building.

His parents named him to honor the prophet,
their child who flew the plane into the building.

This Mohammed was disciple of a Saudi man
whose family had made billions in building.

We all know well how to destroy.
We know that better than we know building.

We have mastered mass destruction—dreamed it,
forged it in the heart of a five-walled building.

How much could we destroy before we see
each temple, mosque, or church is just a building?

Built to serve those who cut loss, build profit,
two towers bore the name of just one building.

When building Babel, people spoke inscrutable tongues.
It's getting close to Ramadan. The hum of prayers is building.

WHAT THEY'RE DOING

They're bulldozing the cheap apartments
where the young Chinese couple were slaughtered
on Veterans Day. They're hauling away broken,
blood-stained bricks. They're making business decisions.
They're making children who will piss in the river
and ride their new bicycles down the center of the street
on Christmas day, grinning, baring sharp little teeth.
They're taking children to church and singing hymns.
They're becoming Christian soldiers, marching as to war.
They're carrying a cross before them like a scythe.
They're entering holy cities in armored personnel carriers.
They're accomplishing missions, declaring victory,
saying *amen, amen,* meaning *so be it, so be it.* And so it is.

CHRISTINA SESTINA

Christina has written a sestina, and it's astonishing that she would hazard becoming forever *Christina Sestina*, nominal identification with that most artificial form. She should have known that writing a sestina is madness, should have stuck to free verse and saved herself, saved her name, kept herself hidden. In a sestina, nothing can ever be hidden. Everything is as plain and obvious as Christina the Astonishing waking at her funeral Mass and floating, saved, to the rafters of the church's ceiling. That's what writing a sestina will get you—levitation and a gawking crowd. Madness may be given order, but not by that ridiculous form. Christina must have torn at her brain, her hair, trying to form ideas to fit refrain words and math, trying to keep hidden the artifice, the arbitrary positioning in the mind, the madness of such a pattern. 123456, 615243. It's astonishing how each progressive stanza of the sestina can record the implosion of the mind, whether saved in a computer file or recorded on paper. Christina may have saved refrain words for weeks only to drop them into a form that collapses of its own weight and design. The sestina falls into itself, 615243, as some people do, to keep themselves hidden, as was the case with Christina the Astonishing, who would hide in ovens or cupboards, the patron saint of madness. She would also roll in fire and stand in icy water, her own madness on display, her faith that, despite every pain, she would be saved by a god she could not see. And that's the astonishing thing, that some of us will suffer hell on earth and be content to form prayers and supplications for a god who is always hidden, who may be gone, who may have always been as artificial as a sestina. What desperate measures we sometimes turn to—writing a sestina or offering words just as coldly chosen to a god—in order to fight the madness of the truth. Everything collapses. Nothing is hidden. Playing with words and math and the idea of gods, no one is saved. Up above this stinking world, the firmament is without form. Christina Sestina cannot become Christina the Astonishing. That's the mad and sad truth, Christina—astonishing in its depth of madness—that a random sestina will do as much as prayer to get us saved, that every time we try to give this life a form, all form stays hidden.

GOD

Somewhere beneath 125th Street there's a small machine
so important that crowds gather, as if around a fire,
just to hear its tiny engine hum, to feel its modest warmth.
Upon this small machine, it seems, everything depends.
When it breaks down, the people look around, wait in silence
for the repairman to appear and convert their anxiety
to awe. They watch in reverence as he begins to massage
the machine back to life with his wrenches and oils.
Even the child peeking from behind her mother's peacoat
seems transfixed. From somewhere down the tunnels
comes a faint chorus of angelic voices that sounds
just the slightest bit like the whir of wheels on rails.

When the engine begins to purr again, the crowd applauds.
But I can't say whether it's out of admiration or relief.
And I can't say what the small machine really does.
The story would be better if the repairman were blind.
Maybe he is. I'm getting most of this from hearsay.
I suppose it could all be made up. But don't you love
the idea of the repairman? And don't you hope
he's trained a promising young apprentice?

GHAZAL FOR CHILDREN

Do you see the anthills and the child?
Now watch the child be a child.

Some chose to leap instead of burn.
Did they find as they fell the joy of a child?

No one could say whether he leapt or burned,
that man whose wife was carrying their first child.

In Manhattan and Mecca, men pray to gods
when their wives are with child.

Decades ago and a world away, nineteen women
gave birth. Each nursed a child.

Maybe there could be another life, another world.
Let us make that world with the mind of a child.

Let us see the leapers rise, not fall. See them float away
like dandelion spores on the breath of a child.

THE GODS HAVE GIVEN UP ON IMMORTALITY

They have.
The palliative
nature of endless life
has been replaced by ceaseless strife.
Now they feel the Cumaean Sybil's curse.
To die seemed bad, yet now it seems to live is worse.
Eternal life appears a god's gift, not a divine hex,
but looks can be deceiving, yes? They got tired of the sex.
Familiarity bred contempt. They sought new loves
until all loves were spent. They tried, like doves,
to mate for life. They failed. Desire
still burns its hellish fire
in each god's eye.
They die.

WHAT EVERYONE KNOWS

My student wants to know what a dragoon is,
and I don't know, but take a stab and say,
It's like an infantryman, and later in the day
I look it up and learn that a dragoon
is a heavily armed, mounted European soldier.
I think about how close the word is to *dragon*
and wonder if there's some connection there,
imagining lots of armor and weaponry atop a horse,
the whole thing breathing fire, metaphorically speaking.
And then I want to see what the difference is
between one of these and an infantryman.

So I look up *infantry* and see that they're
foot soldiers, trained for fighting on foot,
and for the first time I notice the word *infant*
within *infantry* and feel stupid for never
having seen it before. And I see the French root,
in fact, does mean *boy soldier*. Then I think
how adamant we have always been to feed our young
to the battlefield, having watched again the scroll
of nineteen-year-old dead soldiers' names
on my television last night. And now I see the words
Adam and *ant* in *adamant*, and think, from the beginning,
from the garden, we have crushed each other like insects.
And now I know I've got the faculty of association
going and am pleased, though I wonder if it's enough,
if that's all that poets are really meant to do.

Coleridge believed association was at the heart
of it, thought that the secondary imagination
was the working of the esemplastic power
which blends all diverse things into unity.

And this is an apt association too, I guess,
since Coleridge's utterly stupid boyish decision
to join the light dragoons is what brought up
my student's question in the first place.
I suppose *adamant* might just as easily have led me
to Adam and the Ants, the campy '80s pop band
from England (where Coleridge had joined the dragoons).
The lead singer, Adam Ant, would sometimes wear
fanciful epaulets, military garb you might imagine
decorating the shoulders of an eighteenth-century dragoon,
perhaps Silas Tomkyn Comberbache, martial pseudonym
of one Samuel Taylor Coleridge. And now pop music
leads me to think of the Association, that band
who in 1967 asked listeners lots of questions,
but provided only one answer: *Everyone knows
it's Windy.* My friend Wendy truly *hates* that song,
enough to punch me if I start singing it to her.
Wendy lives in Pennsylvania, too far away to punch me now.
I'm in South Carolina, playing around with language again,
trying to diffuse, dissipate, and recreate, to fuse into unity
with that magical power of the imagination, as adept
at this as Coleridge was at military service, I fear.
It's windy outside, everyone knows it, and somewhere
the Association is on the airwaves while infants are dying.

Alone.
The telephone
crouched, not waiting to ring.
Feeling the still air. Listening
to A *Pagan Day*. The catastrophic
wave a full year old. No words, no apostrophic
hymn, no song. No singer. The eddies of the Waccamaw
like the thick flow of time, like resistance, a design flaw.
The day feeling short. In the Hubble's distant stare,
the pale light of new galaxies' faint glare.
A dead Sri Lankan's orphaned son
with eyes as blank as stone.
Like everyone,
alone.

Two

AUBADE

The fuck-
ing sun has struck
its light upon the blinds,
and my nostalgic dream unwinds,
and we're no longer fucking, and I'm sad.
I wake alone. You've gone back to the *Dunciad*.
To say we used to fuck is not wholly true. At least I
tried to make love, to blend my soul with yours, and with you fly—
like doves. To me, at least, it wasn't just a trick.
But you left. And now any Tom or Dick
seems good enough for you. I lie
this dawn, dreaming what I
most want to do:
fuck you.

GLORIA PATRI

He is and always will be
my damned father.

What glory, damnation.
What glory in beginning, end.

To have made someone like me.

To have made me
to unmake him.

A THEATER NEAR YOU

They say the end is coming, coming soon.
They're making preparations, learning how
to sound a droning dirge or victory tune.

They say that grace has made their souls immune,
while other faiths their lord will not allow.
They say the end is coming. Coming soon

to opening night or matinee afternoon,
a final cut: *Apocalypse Right Now.*
To sound a droning dirge or victory tune,

their angels clear dry throats, prepare to croon
a soundtrack for a final holy row.
They say the end is coming, coming soon,

to battlefields already littered, strewn
with severed limb, with child, with olive bough.
To sound a droning dirge or victory tune,

they point to cryptic scripture, ancient rune,
divine approval of their bloody vow.
They say the end is coming, coming soon,
and sing a droning dirge, their victory tune.

INFAMY

Another miserable failure. And now
the heart he sought is floating on the waves
while the *Arizona* settles in the silt.
Tomorrow morning the water will be still
and the heart washed up on the sand.
This day should live in his memory,
but he never remembers the failures,
only hard sobbing, a numb face.
He should try harder to remember.
He should doubt his love for the emperor.
Over the vast Pacific, far from land,
he should consider the innocents
and cut his engines. He should sing
only to himself as he descends like a gull
to crush or drown his kamikaze heart.

GHAZAL OF AIR

What is that acrid smell in the air?
There is no answer in the air.

All flights are grounded. Where jets would slice
through clouds with knifelike wings, nothing is in the air.

The day is so quiet our ears feel numb.
There are no rumbling engines in the air.

Is this a silence that will never be broken?
All words now seem like a waste of air.

The televangelist was screaming about lost souls
when a system's shrill drone broke in and filled the air.

A dragonfly seems more to float than fly—
a perfectly indifferent god of air.

What could I believe in today?
There are no engines in the air.

All foundations gone, none left to build.
No floor beneath us, we'll have to dance on air.

EXEUNT VOLTEMAND AND CORNELIUS

In that, and all things, we will show our duty.
—*Hamlet*, act I, scene ii

Dutiful souls, and dullards, they too are dead.
Enlisted as question carriers in the first act
and in the second bringing answers to the royal stage
of Denmark's king, Voltemand and Cornelius live
like Rosencrantz and Guildenstern—for a moment,
seen briefly, following orders, without thought. That's all.

They assure the court they'll do their duty in *all*
things, be good boys, forever faithful till they're dead.
But what's forever when you only get a moment
or two under the lights? And what's duty but to act
like an automaton, brainless? Who wants to live
like that, another's whim your only reason to be on stage?

Imagine Voltemand seething inside, itching to stage
a rebellion, to insist that he is someone, after all,
not just a pawn to be moved. *I want to live!*
he wants to shout. But then he knows he'll end up dead,
free will or no, and so the feeling passes. He'll act
as he's expected to, quell urges to think beyond the moment.

Imagine Cornelius staring, open-mouthed, in the moment
alone, no thought of past or future, only the dusty stage
beneath his feet on his mind. He's seen it all before, each act
just like the last. The rat that scurries under the curtain is all
he cares about. He wants to hide behind an arras too, end up dead,
not for the lines, but just not to have tomorrow to live.

Picture the two of them backstage, finished, all live
action just a murmur from the other side, their one moment
done with three acts to go. Do they just sit there, picking at dead
skin and toenails and old wounds? Or do they debate which stage
of grief is the worst, maybe whether they're really there at all?
What's the difference between existential thought and act?

Think back to a time when you could have, but did not act.
What difference did it make? Or could it have made? Can you live
with that? It's clear you do. But are you happy, really, at all?
Please excuse the poem's strange, accusatory turn for a moment.
It's not personal, just philosophical. Listen: This is the only stage
you'll ever have. Do something worth your life before you're dead.

In Stoppard's *Rosencrantz and Guildenstern Are Dead*, two dolts act
as if all the world is just a stage, as if there's no real reason to live.
Not true. You'll have your moment. We all do. The readiness is all.

ANECDOTE OF THE PLATE

for the young woman with the vanity license plate CARRION

I passed a car in Tennessee,
expecting Goth kid with sulking stare,
but what I got was more flower child,
a college-aged girl with brilliant smile

who was singing along to something
(Widespread Panic? Phish? The Dead?)
as if the music were distilled joy.
She turned and waved as I passed.

She wanted me to persevere, I guess,
as I guess she'd tried to pledge herself.
The Y had been taken when she applied,
and so she'd settled for the I instead.

It took dominion in my head.
She hadn't been saying that she'd be dead
someday, though she will, as will you and me
and everything else in Tennessee.

AFTERLIFE

But don't worry . . . you will someday.
—final line of *American Beauty* (1999)

You will.
That is, until
the charged battery drains
and everything dissipates, wanes,
falls out of sight and meditative thought.
Until then, you'll have some answers: that all you bought
is gone, that all you did is done, that every breath is blown.
While brain impulses fade, you'll see this life was not your own
nor anyone else's. You'll finally understand
what the murdered man meant. Life is brief and
beautiful as a blood-red rose.
Resist resistance throes.
Try to be still,
tranquil.

KEEN & KOAN

A woman is keening across the cove
as if to hear her own voice taking flight
over the water. Not a howl or moan,
not a bellow, but a fine keen, hard-edged

and clear, the sound of grieving perfected.
What is the feel of mourning in the throat?
What is the sound of a dead man weeping?
I have to call her wordless cry a keen

but have to question, too, what I'm hearing
from across the cove. Is her keen a song?
Can grieving be turned into an art form?
Can it carve the stone as well as the soul?

I'm growing tired of meditation.
What's the sound of a woman's voice miming?
What is the water to the empty boat?
My mind can never shake meditation,

can't escape involuntary brooding
over meaning in a meaningless life,
trying to achieve momentary stays
against confusion, desperation, fear.

Or listening obsessively to the night.
Is this hearing the same thing as knowing?
Is truth buried in sound beyond the mind?
You are keen, my lord, says dour Ophelia,

sick of jokes. O lord of this other world,
you are keen, as well, dangling these dark koans
in my mind, not letting me go. That keen
still rides across the cove. Lord, it is sharp.

DECLARING A DRAW

Three pawns, two rooks, and a couple of kings
wait for the end on a flat field of play

where every shade of gray has been distilled
to a harsh symmetry of black and white,

where queens have been sacrificed, knights slaughtered,
bishops forgotten like all their dead creeds.

A cold, quiet field where none still standing
can even remember how war began.

From this height, I can see my father's house
below—distant, remote, a tiny hell

in which he dwells, from which I somehow climbed.
He sits in his den, playing solitaire.

My sister sits on her worn, lonely bed
upstairs, smoking, watching television,

and trying to will an end to her life.
My mother has escaped into the ground.

The house feels small in my mind, looks smaller
from this height. It's lost so much of its weight

I can almost think I never felt it
bearing down on my chest. I called it home

those heavy years. I used to walk alone
in that backyard and dream another life

in which I was an orphaned only child
who had discovered an unlikely cure

for death. But I'd have to go back inside
when it was time for dinner or for bed.

I was taught to feel ashamed for wanting
something more, using imagination

to reach for it. My father once told me
something that his grandfather had told him:

*If you have nothing to do, it's better
to dig holes in your yard and refill them*

than to do nothing at all. I heard that
and tried to dig to China with my mind.

He told me other things: how I should run
away from him as quickly as I could

if he ever saw me with a black girl,
how the poor had richly earned poverty

with their laziness, how his creator
had laid down natural laws that he knew well.

My silent nods were a makeshift defense,
a castling of the soul, a strategy.

And now he sits alone inside that house
that's smaller and smaller from this distance

of years. He plays solitaire every night
just like he did for years before I left.

Once, when I'd discovered chess, he told me
that he thought checkers was the better game.

*They have mapped out every possible move
in chess,* he said. *But every checkers game*

is different. I tried to teach him, made him
play a game. Three quick moves: Fool's Mate. He shook

his head in silence. I only felt loss.
I left. I wish I hadn't had to leave

my mother and my sister there. I wish
it could have been different, know it couldn't.

Sometimes a novice will use the wrong term
for draw, call it *stalemate.* This is a draw,

Father. I'm not going to move, though I could.
There's no clock in this game. I'm going to watch

from this distance in the awful silence
you taught me. No one is trapped or pinned here.

And there's nothing but time waiting to pass.
There's nothing like victory, nothing like loss.

SOME OTHER DAY

> *Someday I'm gonna make her mine.*
> —final line of *Abbey Road* (1969)

Someday I'll find the perfect set of words.
I'll murmur them into her tender ear
and tongue the lobe for luck, for good measure.
Then she'll be clichéd putty in my hands.
We'll walk along a path, listen to birds
make loving, wordless songs. I'll feel no fear.
We'll make a wordless song of our pleasure—
I'll twist my fingers in her hair's fine strands,
and she'll whisper the name that's not a name.
And as we lie together then, she'll say,
I've always wanted this. Why did you wait?
That's when I'll think of everything I'll miss.
I'll swallow shame, and I won't look away.
It's late. I'm dying. Give me one more kiss.

Is this:
It could be bliss.
Meursault's mother said that
anything can become old hat
and will, given enough time. Even hell.
You would adapt, you know. And then (why not?) do well
down there amidst the brimstone, fire, and ash. You're hot, my dear.
You'd rule that damned scene. Your ass could make Satan quake with fear,
each breast could strike ten minor demons dumb, those lips
that formed *goodbye* (my own apocalypse)
could give icy commands. Your heart
could freeze the hottest part
of anywhere.
Go there.

Three

INSIDE

In the lake, the cottonmouth. In the sea, the shark.
In the soil, the growing seed. In the tree, the lark.

In the dark, the insects' call. In the light, the trust.
In the child, the weight of years. In the steel, the rust.

In the dust, the memory. In the air, your soul.
In my head, the unsaid words. In the diamond, coal.

In the hole, your polished box. In the earth, the quake.
In my blood, your vessel ran. In these lines, its wake.

NO BEGINNING

The pantoum always ends with its beginning.
—from a professor's discarded notes

In this end is no beginning
though you still live as if it's so
and spend your days avoiding sinning,
thinking you have some place to go.

Though you still live as if it's so,
there's no beginning at the end.
Thinking you have some place to go,
you always fear most to offend.

There's no beginning at the end.
There's not a spring after the fall.
You always fear most to offend
a god that's not there after all.

There's not a spring after the fall
of all those answers long believed.
A god that's not there after all
cannot be willed, not be retrieved.

To all those answers long believed
you cling as if your very lives
cannot be willed, not be retrieved.
But in the end a truth arrives.

You live as if entire lives
must be spent avoiding sinning.
But in the end a truth arrives:
in that end there's no beginning.

THE DAYS OF OUR LIVES

They sawed off the bottom of the hourglass
sometime around 1860. They used
a glass saw made with bright, hard-edged diamonds
(millennia to make those tiny teeth!)

and sheared the thing clean off. And ever since,
people have been leaping into the void,
emitting Pekingese yelps, stretching out
fingers, grasping for each sharp, tumbling grain.

FINAL FANFARE

> *Go, bid the soldiers shoot.*
> —final line of *Hamlet* (circa 1601)

Bid them
sing an anthem
to a flat dead march tune
to mark these ends that come too soon.
You come most carefully upon your hour,
Francisco jokes. But late or early, we know our
time is coming, so bid the soldiers shoot again. And bray
the trumpets, sound the kettle drum. Yes, let the fading day
be filled with wine and laughter and, by God, with guns
to shake the sky and make the dying sun's
last rays tremble over the dead.
There's nothing to be said,
so let's expire
with fire.

ARS POETICA

It's not a perfect world, Mother, but you died
at home, without thought, in little or no pain,
better than most. Still, if I could change it, I would

take some things away. I would take away the dribble
of half-chewed food that fell down your chin
from your open mouth like a thick tear.

I would take you out of your chair
at the breakfast table and put you back in bed,
would make you sleep. I would take away

the last morning you woke up in that house,
would take away the house, but leave
the wind chimes that you loved to hear

in spring. I would take away the illness
from your brain, would take my ill sister away.
I would erase my silence, erase my words,

make years disappear. I would not insist
on cross-dressing for Halloween when I was six,
wailing and kicking the back of the driver's seat

until you wheeled the car back into the parking space
and returned to the counter at Roses Discount Store
to exchange the ghost costume you'd chosen

for the wicked witch I wanted to be.
I would be a ghost for you, Mother.
I would fade away into another past.

It's just another thing you'd never know.
I would not let you take that first step
down into the mouth of the cave.

You would meet a kinder man in 1946.
I wouldn't be there for you, Mother. I never was.
I'm not here now. This is another world

where you can smell gardenias, watch cardinals
at the feeder. Listen—a distant coastal breeze
is playing wind chimes, and you can hear them.

DISORDER

I've been waiting for a guide—for Virgil,
Dante, Jesus Christ, anyone—to take
my hand and show a path through these dark streets.

I've been thinking about the sensation
of touch, of another hand cupped in mine,
a hand not so worn by a rough-edged world,

softer, younger, maybe even my own
from thirty years ago. How would I look
at myself now from then? How would I feel?

I've been thinking about how I should feel
about my sister, about her birth cord
wrapped around her throat, choking forever,

about her solitary days at home.
I've been thinking about family, distance,
what life I might live out. About my death.

I've been thinking about thinking too much,
about rote movement as alternative,
just keeping myself going like a shark

that swims to breathe, evading conscious thought.
I step up from the desk and walk around,
but still can't shed the stillness at the core.

I've been walking dark streets of memory,
waiting for a guide to show the way through
the gates of hell's walled city, where shrapnel

litters the parade route and children test
sharp metal with their tongues, where sirens shriek
from dusk to daybreak, where my sister dwells.

I hadn't been born when she tried to breathe.
I couldn't have cut that cord. But the child
now holding my hand tugs at it with guilt.

I've been trying to find my mother's ghost,
wanting to apologize to the air.
I've been trying to see what's never there.

I've been thinking about my father's stare
cutting across the table at breakfast
and boring his frustration and anger

straight into my sister's face as she wiped
the tears that ran from her eyes like two streams,
moving one disintegrating tissue

from left eye to right, unable to stanch
the flow, my mother looking straight ahead
into the blank, silent space between them.

The streets are dark, as are the roads, the paths,
the trails, the untouched fields. I want a guide
to extend a hand, help me take a step

into the air, show me a sunset's light
over the horizon, give me order.
Or, if not order, at least momentum.

If not a path through the woods, then movement.
If not a cure for the soul, then movement.
Just pure thoughtless movement, movement, movement.

YOUR HOME IS AT RISK IF YOU DO NOT
KEEP UP REPAYMENTS

Idiot, slow down. Slow down.
—final line of *OK Computer* (1997)

Slow down
until you drown
in stasis as the world
grinds to a halt, its oceans whirled
around all cities, towns, and villages—
all kings, queens, jokers, stockbrokers, and savages—
and everything's erased, quiet, peaceful, and finally clean,
all dingy urban buildings washed to a metallic sheen.
Slow down, look around, and appreciate the end
that you brought on. And try to apprehend
one more gorgeous, poisoned sunset,
its chemical palette
peeling away
the day.

THESE BE HECTORING LARGE-SCALE VERSES

They fuck us up, the father, son,
and most of all the holy ghost—
that vague idea beyond icon,
a wholly insubstantial host.

But of the fucked we're not the first,
and, God knows, we won't be the last.
Whole generations have been cursed
by phantom words throughout the past.

Men hand a history down to Man—
a ghost-writ volume signed by God.
Its blood-red verses pulse and scan
and mark with stones the fresh-laid sod.

FOR FORGETTING

Forget it, Jake. It's Chinatown.
    —final line of *Chinatown* (1974)

Forget about the sense you tried to make
of family histories, deaths, and cities sold
for profit, turned to ash. Forget it all.
Forget that brothers burn, that sisters drown.
Forget each desert turned into a lake.
Forget the fading stories, all the old
decaying notes you read about the fall.
And take no notes yourself, write nothing down.
It's coming to an end, a final take
on every worthless story ever told.
The great ones are past telling, past recall.
Forget the father's laugh, the daughter's frown.
Your stake in this is done. All trails are cold.
Forget the call. It's time you left this town.

HOLY NIGHT

My father said he wished the child were dead.
He didn't say it in so many words,
but he said it. And it was Christmas Eve.
I breathed in silent tension next to him.

The news anchor said that of the seven
born to a black couple three nights before
the weakest child had gathered strength and would,
the doctors said, most likely now survive.

I'm sorry to hear that, my father hissed.
That's just what this country needs, seven more—
of course he used the word. You know he did.
The television screen blurred to pastels.

I sat in silence next to him, the man
whose blood was my blood, whose eyes looked like mine,
and tried to breathe the thick air between us.
He was my father. This was Christmas Eve.

Lord of this other world, what will you make
of this? And reader, what will you accept?
That I stood up without a word and left
the house, got into my car, and then drove

to the pizza place as he expected
me to, picked up our order, and drove back
to that goddamned house to join my mother
and sister, who'd been singing Christmas hymns

by candlelight at the evening service
while my father wished death upon a child?
Will you accept that I wept on that drive,
listening to Radiohead's "The Tourist,"

wishing I could stop the world's spinning cold,
drive off its surface and take to the sky,
break its gravitational hold, sever
myself from it forever then and there?

Reader, I hear your silence now, hear it
like I heard silence that night in the space
between my father's words and the night sky
I could see through my windshield, one bright star—

impossibly distant, already dead—
pulsing its pure light through millennia
of utter void to meet my aching eyes.
Maybe it's better that you have no words,

that I have no answer. Maybe better
to just recall the peace of that short drive,
its brief respite where music and silence
were one blessing and the dark night holy.

GHAZAL OF DAYS

The networks, of course, were prepared for such a day.
Slick production, theme music, canned interviews filled the day.

The television replays how the television first played it:
a cut-in interrupting Katie Couric on *Today*.

The images seem surreal, seem crafted, seem familiar—
like scenes from *Terminator, Die Hard, Independence Day*.

The same footage rolls every five minutes, and it feels
like it's happening again each time in one unending day.

I don't know why I listened to the Kinks' "Days." It's different now.
It had never sounded like a lament to God before today.

In 1990 *Voyager* turned around to take a photograph
of a pale blue dot rotating in a beam of light to make a day.

Talking heads tell us we'll have to learn to live in a new
and dangerous world. Tomorrow is the twelfth, another day.

IS IT OKAY IF WE DON'T OSCILLATE TONIGHT?

Is it okay if we don't oscillate
between self-forgiveness and self-loathing?
Between the power to change things and fate?
Between simple nakedness and clothing?

Is it okay if the dull pendulum
doesn't swing from one side to the other
tonight? If there's only a steady hum
and sleep and no thoughts of the dead mother?

Could we escape self-scrutiny tonight
and find a tiny precipice of peace?
Is that allowed? Could we shut out the light
and rest our face on our wife's shoulder, please?

Could we, tonight, just listen to the weak,
droning whir of the fan and not its creak?

When I would get a splinter as a child,
my father would strike a match and then hold
one of my mother's thin sewing needles
in the flame until it glowed a bright red,
sanitizing the steel. Then he'd hold me
down and dig into my flesh to retrieve
the shard of wood. When I think of him now,
that's the sweetest image I can recall,
the concentration on his face as he
stabbed at his child's finger or foot, as he
tried to make something right by digging out
what's wrong.
          He used to sneeze in sets of three—
two quick bursts and then a dramatic pause
building suspense before the crescendo
of an enormous third. My sister coughed
the scornful laugh she'd learned from him, mocking
his involuntary functions, the things
he couldn't control, just as he mocked her.
She'd shake her head from side to side and snort.

I had a professor once who told me
that his great-grandfather, a foot soldier
in the Confederate army, survived
three days of hell at Gettysburg and then
came home after the war, got a splinter

in his hand, developed an infection,
and died. Life before antibiotics
was like that: every day a chance to die.

But I guess that applies to any time.

I had another professor who taught
the psychology of aging, a field
that assumes normal life expectancy.
I learned about natural human response
to weakening health, fading memory,
the inevitability of death.
All the things we expect to come on slow.
He returned home for part of the summer
one year to visit his aging parents.
One July morning he went for a jog
around the neighborhood where he'd grown up,
and a woman driving down the same road
sneezed, sneezed so hard that her body shook, sneezed
so hard that she lost control of her car,
and swerved, just briefly, onto the shoulder.
My professor lay there a little while
and then was nowhere at all anymore.

In ancient Greece, sneezes were thought to be
prophetic signs from the gods—good omens,
usually. When a foot soldier answered
the end of Xenophon's speech with a sneeze,
his comrades heard it as a divine cheer,
the gods' guidance to their deliverance.
By the Middle Ages, Europeans
had grown a bit more skeptical, fearing
the sneeze as a potentially fatal

expulsion of the life force. *God bless you,*
they said, thinking divine intervention
would be needed to spare the sneezer's life.

Maybe one of Xenophon's foot soldiers
managed to make it home after the wars
and caught his own death splinter in a thumb
or sneezed himself into oblivion.

Maybe my sister's life could have been good,
happy, if she'd gotten more oxygen
at birth, if her brain hadn't been damaged.
Or if the damage had been great enough
to keep her from understanding her life
too well. Maybe we could have been happy.

The world and time and every life are grand
and very, very small.

                   And sometimes poems
are very, very small, but feel as if
they could do anything. Sometimes I wish
I could turn time backward and say just once
God bless you to my father and mean it.
Go back and tell my mother *I'm sorry.*
Go back to thirteen years before my birth,
to a delivery room, and try to help
untangle a cord. Go back to somewhere
where I'm not, take a needle to this life,
and work at mending, or at digging out.

OUTSIDE

Out of view, more galaxies. Out of time, more light.
Out of sand, the turtle's head. Out of day, the night.

Out of sight, a loving god. Out of love, a son.
Out of song, the nightingale. Out of void, the sun.

Out of running water, life. Out of stagnant, death.
Out of ages past, a poem, pulled up out of breath.

Out of method, futile search. Out of myths untrue.
Out of other worlds, some hope. Out of this one, you.

From this distance he can see that the man
is not Jack Gilbert. And he is not yet himself.
Being himself would not be better than being Gilbert.
Only Gilbert is more than Gilbert. Failure is better
than success in the same way that this poem
is still getting at something as it descends
into parody, elegy, and palimpsest at once.
We die and are put into the earth forever
is a line directly stolen from Gilbert's "Tear It Down."
Putting it in this poem means neither success
nor failure nor larceny. People need to read it
even if its magnitude of beauty is too difficult
for people. When I spoke with Jack on the telephone
to invite him to my university the next fall, he mostly
wanted to talk about my Italian name, to ask about
my poems. He wanted to know what I wanted
from poetry. I said I'd like to say something
to someone born two hundred years from now.
I think he approved, or I may have just heard
his enormously generous spirit smiling.
After his summer in Greece with Linda,
he could not remember ever having talked to me,
told my colleague who called to make travel arrangements
that he had never heard of our university.
Today the woman I love rejected my artificial soul.
What is it we want from poetry? When Jack Gilbert
and I have been put into the earth forever,

what will it mean if someone reads "Tear It Down" or
"Years and Years and Years Later"? Is there still time
to insist? Let my heart be feral, too wild for every
woman I love. This poem, Jack, is as helpless
as crushed birds, and still I say with you, nevertheless.

Nor the limbs, nor the leaves,
nor the arms, the legs.
Nor the long-lived, nor short-,
nor the quick, the dead.
Nor Isaac, nor Ishmael,
nor Milton, Donne.
Nor poem, nor song,
nor scripture, call.
Nor the peach, nor the pit,
nor flower, seed.
Nor mother, nor father,
nor sister, child.
Nor poles, nor caps,
nor water, ice.
Nor Jim, nor Jeff,
nor Ian, Kurt.
Nor the future, John.
Nor the future, Sid.
No future, no future,
no future for us.